Keith Ravenscroft is married with four grown-up children and three grandchildren. He studied English Literature (with an admixture of Philosophy) at Cambridge University and then spent most of his working life as a writer and creative director in advertising agencies in the UK and North America.

From a position of hardline atheism, Keith gradually came to faith in his middle years and trained as a Lay Minister in the Church of England. He has been engaged in preaching, teaching, and leading worship since 2007.

He and his wife Avril, a graphic artist and now an Anglican priest, have worked together as well as lived together for many years and during that time have been residents in Canada and Italy, as well as in the UK.

Apart from music, Keith's great passions are Philosophical Theology and Christian Spirituality as expressed within the writings of poets and mystics throughout the ages.

*These poems are dedicated
to my beloved Avril
who has loved and supported me
for so many years,
with grace and commitment
that go way beyond any words
with which I could even begin
to thank her.*

Keith Ravenscroft

STUMBLINGS

AUSTIN MACAULEY PUBLISHERS™

LONDON • CAMBRIDGE • NEW YORK • SHARJAH

A CIP catalogue record for this title is available from the British Library.

ISBN 9781398495753 (Paperback)
ISBN 9781398495760 (Hardback)
ISBN 9781398495784 (ePub e-book)
ISBN 9781398495777 (Audiobook)

www.austinmacauley.com

First Published 2023
Austin Macauley Publishers Ltd®
1 Canada Square
Canary Wharf
London
E14 5AA

A big thank you to my dear family who have always supported my efforts. I especially want to thank Reverends Rob Green and Sue Hawkins and Professor Robert Boyd for their encouragement and perceptiveness whenever I shared a thought with them.

Table of Contents

Introduction

I've called this collection of poems *Stumblings* because that's what they are. They are mainly attempts to ask and answer questions, confront confusions, hold onto hope, express joys, sorrows, pain, and above all love. A few of them are role plays, as I try to imagine what it would be like to be someone else – my great aunt locked in dementia or an abandoned lover in a mental meltdown for instance.

All of these poems were written with my dear family and some friends in mind, and always and preeminently to energise myself for new attempts to understand and accept what my life has brought me. So in all of them, I wrestle to come to terms with what it means even to exist, and I strive to comprehend the God I believe in, but whom I so consistently fail to connect with as deeply as I long to do.

I have always been a writer of one kind or another. But my writing of poetry seems to have been accelerated by two huge life events. The first is the sudden cataclysmic blindness of my beloved Avril. The second is the horror of the COVID pandemic. Both of these have caused me to question with new urgency, and yet to reaffirm, so much in life. The result is poems of anguish, of faith, of questions that seem to defy answering. But thankfully also poems of joy and fulfilment that ultimately overcome all doubt and despair.

I have no egotistical illusions about anything I have written, but for what it is worth, everything here is what I care about, what I question, what I believe and who I am. I hope these 'Stumblings' will be accepted in that spirit by whoever may read them.

Keith Ravenscroft
November 2021

As Though I Have My Life
to Live Again

Like sitting out the last dance
That's how it feels right now
As if the things I lived close up
I just see from afar
All the passions all the love
And the help from God above
Are like a precious memory to me now.

It's only when I look back
And run the film again
I seem to see the meaning
The rumour of a plan
All the pleasure all the pain
Comes rushing through my heart again
And everyone I've loved is with me now.

All the pleasure all the pain
Comes rushing through my heart again
As though I had my life to live again.

The woman who changed everything
The wisdom that she brought

The quickening of passion
The sharing of a thought
The little lives that followed
Not all ours, simply borrowed
She showed me what it meant to love again.
The struggle to make sense of things
When all around seemed grim
The stumbles, the epiphanies
A presence like a hymn
The voice that interceded
With the message that I needed
Saying I had to seize my life, and live it all again.

All the pleasure all the pain
Comes rushing through my heart again
And everything I've loved is with me now.

All the pleasure all the pain
Comes rushing through my heart again
As if I have a new life to begin.

Bursting into Light

Locked out of sight
Consigned to live in darkness.
Deprived of what was sweet.
The clattering wings of wheeling birds
The dancing waves,
The shimmering of heat.

The hands that drew,
Coaxed beauty from a line,
Still touch my heart
Still show your love is mine.
Now hesitant, still loving, and so gentle
More like the tremulous falling of a petal.

The face of Christ in Florence and Siena,
The hilltop towns, the mountains and the sea
A precious loss that memory holds together
While I who never saw what you could see
Hold a poor remnant of what used to be.
All now, without your insights, so much less to me

Yet much remains for you my wounded healer
The praise you bring, the message that you give

Lights other lives though yours is so much darker
Telling of bliss to come and love to live.
As if your sorrows turned to others' joys,
The silent suffering – transformed into triumphal noise.

But this won't be reality forever
I pray and hope, believing at the end
Within that place where loss is just a memory
The blind shall see, the broken lives shall mend.
And dawn will come, the ending of your night
With all its darkness bursting into light.

Iambic Agonies

The unshakeable grammar
Of iambic pentameter
Has kept poets in thrall
From the great to the small.
As each sweats to compress
Each thought they possess
Into syllables prescribed
For the dead and the live;
Scribblers like them
When they pick up their pen.

It gave Shakespeare his edge
As he drove a great wedge
Through our small expectation
Of verse that must stay con-
signed to the rigour
Of lines never bigger
Than what is prescribed
By the pulse and the drive
Of accents familiar
And thoughts that are similar
Through poetic convention.
Though they crack with the tension

Of risking derision
In their self-imposed prison.

While they cling like a limpet
To rules that could permit it
To flow like a deep-bedded
Stream of invention.
If only they woke and paid
Total attention.

So what can help this struggling old man
Who wrestles still to fit the thoughts he can
Into the mould iambic verse prescribes
That clips the wings of poets through their lives?

If I can't float my thoughts upon its wing
Then how the hell can I write anything?

A Way of Happening, a Mouth

I breathe out thought in order of some kind
Making a sequence left upon a page.
Yet nothing seems to change except the page.
Nothing happens.

I wrestle with a rhyme, then set in train
A cadence that may fully underline
The latest point I'm struggling to make.
Except there may not even be a point.

I try my best to shun the obvious,
Only to fall in some deep cliche pit.
In my attempts to be accessible
I just traduce the theme to make it fit.

Some other people read what I may write
Though not too many
Some even claim to like the finished verse
Others, like me, are not too sure about it.
So am I just as Shakespeare would describe it
Wrapping the truth 'within my rawer breath'?
And should the rest be only silence

As what we hear in Hamlet's dying words?

Yes but then no. Despite the daunting odds
Something evolves minutely through the writing
A way of happening that may lack precision.
Provisional. Almost too small to notice.

And sadly ready to be chased away
By the reality of flesh and blood
That is true life.

Yet sometimes the words I write have more than just
A paper-thin existence.
They may not have the power to change our world
But I can feel they somehow do change mine.

800 Years

Eight hundred years of praise and prayer
Voices that never cease
Still centre of a changing world
Speaking of calm and peace.

Eight hundred years of holy calm
Set in a bower of green
Surrounded by the graves of those
Whose lives can be no longer seen.

Patiently there in times of peace
A sign of hope in war
The memory of all those souls
Who have gone on before.

And some whose stone memorials
Have vanished over time
Whose names are lost, except to God
Who is immune to time.

Inside our church God's music swells
The words of Christ still spoken
As they have been by spirits who seem
Still present as a token

Of permanence, of values held
Outside the frame of time
A living witness to the power
Of holiness enshrined.
So, here for us a place of rest
But also of renewal
Where lives are lived,
And deaths are blessed

By those who come to celebrate
The joys and griefs the years possess
Baptism, wedding, funeral
The story of Salvation,
Life winning over death

Eight hundred years, a place that holds
The meaning of our lives.
For those who lived and those who died
Throughout those long-lost centuries

Are still a part of you and me.
And so St Peter's holds the key
To who we've been, and who we are
And who we long to be.

It's Only the Music That's Crying, Not Me

I don't want a drink and I don't want to talk
I move like a child that is learning to walk
The sound of the speakers is hurting my mind
And I've lost what I had and it's nowhere to find
I forgot how to feel and my senses are blind
And I don't trust your hand though your voice is still kind

(refrain)

While the pianist pleads and the saxophone throbs
And the bass player's racked with a spasm of sobs
I look through the mirrors that cover this place
And I see what is there but I can't see my face
And I want to be gone and I wish I was free
And it's only the music that's crying, not me

You're not like my husband you're more like her lover
She knows where you're at and you're there for each other
You say that she has what's important to you
I never had that and I know that it's true
But I cannot accept though you tell me each time
That you're going with her and you used to be mine.

(repeat refrain)

I'll go home tonight to the same empty bed
With nothing to hold but the hurt in my head
It's hard to recall just what loving was like
When we kissed and combined in the warmth of the night
And you'll be with her in a bed that's not mine
With her love and your passion to soften your pain.

(final refrain)

While the pianist pleads and the saxophone throbs
And the bass player's racked with a spasm of sobs
I look through the mirrors that cover this place
And I see what is there but I can't see my face
And I want to be gone and I wish I was free
And it's only the music that's crying, not me

Running Out of Room

I've no more room in my head

Not for concepts.
Not for precepts.

Nowhere left to think in.
Just no more room.

No more stoking the fires
of factitious knowledge

Nothing new to be used
and saved up for
that rainy day that never comes.

I've run right out of headspace
and now it rains only emptiness
every day.

I used to find room for everything
that floated into my head
I'd suck up knowledge and opinions
like a mental hoover.

One that's now disconnected.

What is the point of all those points
we make to score over each other?

Yet silence is not always wisdom either
It can mask the kind of foolishness
that we often mistake for profundity

when we should know that deep down
we're just inhabiting a mental vacuum
that only offers the illusion of meaning.

The only meaning I'm sure about
nowadays is the absence of meaning.
The void with which
I fill my empty days.

No longer valuing what I know.
Knowing instead that it may only
be worth the less than nothing
that other people
dismiss it as.

I've run out of room
to fill up my head with.

So now I'm left
brooding on vacant emptiness.

'Every Word Is
an Unnecessary Stain
on Silence'

(Samuel Beckett)

Silent Creation.
A stirring into life.

Out of nothing
Out of nowhere.

Willed, loved, into Being.
In the beginning

was the Word.
But not just any word.

Your Creating Word.

The holy word
that broke the solemn
silence of eternity.

With thoughts to manifest
and love to share.

Never meant merely to fuel
the vacuous mutterings
with which we have squandered
this your greatest gift.
Meant rather as a sign of life
a mark of being there.
Alive. Sentient. Capable.

Of more than just a storm of spittle
drowning and besmirching
the Word and the face of God.

As we mostly dare to use it.

When we have been given
the power to voice our worship,
Promises to speak

In thanks for your gift
we mostly only utter
lies with which we stain
the sanctity of what You offered us.

We're especially adept at this.

Lord forgive us for our blasphemies
our casual collusions

For using words
to stifle truth
Your Word, your truth.

Bring us to you through
that still small voice.

Calling us more urgently
than any merely human words
could do.

Then wash away the stains
that we are stained with
and let our rest be silence.

A Dying Fall: Reflections on the French Baroque

A dying fall
That's what they called this sound
Music that seems to celebrate
Its own approaching end.
Expressing all the dignity of grief.

Spoken through tongues and keyboards
In ruminating, quiet courtliness
And uncomplaining submission to its fate.
Sounding reserved, with all the surface politesse
Of Louis' limiting courtly conventions.

Yet deep, so deep.
As if consumed by inner knowledge
Condemned to be smothered
as soon as it was born.
Whispered, not spoken out loud.
For fear of self-disclosure in the notes.

Unlike the confident harmonies of faith
We know from Bach.
Or the flickering Spanish sunshine of Scarlatti.
Here we are only privileged to hear
A low-lit chiaroscuro of ambiguity
As if each note foretold yet contradicted
It's own inevitable cessation.
Yet these in their constrained and sober singing
Invite a leap into the musical abyss.
Their dying fall resounds then safely reaches
The eternal arms that wait to gather in
All those who worship through their music's offering.

Whose dying fall shall rise to life with God.

It's a Long Way to Eternity

Some folks believe there's a clear simple road
And to follow the path is a trouble free ride,
But some of us carry a wearisome load
And can't tell if we'll get to the other side.

What can it mean that we don't know now?
Where can we go if we don't know how?
Baffled, benighted, it's tempting to fall
Too overburdened even to crawl.

(1st Chorus)

'Cause it's a long way to eternity
So much to hope for, for you and for me
Life can look dark when we so long to see
Weighing us down, till we get to break free.

Is it our past that won't loosen its grip?
Is it the struggle to rise when we slip?
Maybe the answer is clear after all
Maybe all Christians must stumble and fall.

(Repeat 1st Chorus: Because it's a long way to eternity…)

Someone came to us who did understand
The need for forgiveness the warmth of a hand
The path we can follow, the strength to go on
The hope for things better in the place he has gone.

(Final Chorus)

So stumbling and staggering, but still moving on
We shall, at the last day, be warmed by the Son
When we get to the place that his sacrifice won
And the way to eternity is travelled and done.

Beyond All Imagining

'There is in God, some say,
A deep but dazzling darkness'

(Henry Vaughan)

'God is that which we have
not yet understood'

(Rowan Williams)

Two elliptical responses to
Our failure to know
the unknowable.

There seems to be a darkness
we are incapable of getting beyond.
A reality that we can sense
but not identify.
Something that seems to cover
itself and us in perplexity.

Leaving us empty, yet aware
that somehow there may be

a plenitude beyond
the seeming starvation
of absent longing.

But sadly it seems
that everything remains
permanently, achingly,
beyond our reach.
However hard
we strain and search.
Ever hopeful as we may be
despite our inability
to comprehend
or even catch a glimpse,
of what it is that we are missing.

It's not a comforting conclusion
to come to. It leaves us with
a stultifying question.
Are we actually encountering the absolute
by virtue of its seeming absence?
Or merely imagining the whole thing?

Is the totality of our reality
simply in the imagined control of
a Being who has no reality?
Leaving us crying out
from our own emptiness
into an even greater emptiness?

And yet this presence beyond
absence, even in their times
of utmost dereliction, has been
leaned on for strength
by the most resolute
of minds and hearts.

Some of them have actually dared
to save their lives by losing them.
Running into the jaws
of wild beasts
rather than submitting to
the even sharper weapons
of the cruel, uncomprehending
enemies who have always run things.

Believing in things not seen.
Even at the moment of death.

But as for us:
our logical minds now,
like those of their tormentors then,
recoil from anything we fail to understand.
So we weave our rationales,
propound our petty proof texts.

Hoping to make things
comprehensible,
simpler to control –
and God reassuringly smaller.

And so we comfort ourselves
with the paltriest human misconceptions
of what salvation might look like.
Elbowing our unenlightened selves
Into the centre of a story in which
we ourselves become the heroes
or maybe even the villains.

For us it doesn't really seem
to matter which we are,
provided history sings along
to the song we have composed.
But maybe it is healthier to surrender
a struggle we can never win.
And wait to be enfolded and received
within that 'deep but dazzling darkness'
that is God's eternal home
and some day may be ours.

A Doorway into Thanks

Lord I don't know what to say
is how my pathetic prayers usually start.

If prayer is a contest
I've already lost.

But if our words are meant to be
no more than a creaking doorway
into God then I already
have his attention.

I imagine him listening patiently
wrapped in my failure to say
to pray what it is I would
have Him hear.

Observing my pointless pain
sweating to remind him of what
he has always known.
Who reads all things all people
like a child's book.

So why even try?

Why tie in knots what is not
to be said with any kind
of victory?

Why not simply approach
his silence in silence
imitate a small part of
his voiceless greatness?

Traduced by our words
locked in by our desperate
urge for fluency
we wound what we should only worship.

And yet it's hard to know
what else is left to us to do

Only a kind of defeated silence
Or at best a voice
that can simply stutter haltingly
of the love that seems impossible
to express or live?

Not much. But maybe something that
at best is better than just nothing.

Though nothing like as good as simply listening.
Even if all we hear is silence

And God's silence is louder
than any words of ours.

On the far side of the doorway
there lives a speaking presence
beyond all knowing all description.

This voice will only truly speak to us
out of the surrounding silence

When we're content to let it overwhelm
those faltering words that we so fruitlessly
stumble to say.

Living in the Shadows
of My Mind

It's always there whatever I may do
Beside my body, almost out of view
It lurks around me, undermining
All the self I'm far from finding
Until I hardly know now who I am.

I'm living in the shadows of my mind
Where any self I had seems left behind.
Just shadow where a shadow shouldn't be
That's really there, but isn't really me.

If I forget, it still remembers me
It smothers me, although I think I'm free
It haunts my dreams, it fills my days,
It kills my will and stifles praise
So that I hardly know, now, what I am.

I'm living in the shadows of my life
Where apathy conflicts with inner strife
And what I think my mind believes
Is torn away and only leaves
A hollow space, in which I just survive.

I reach for heaven but plummet underground
And any prayer I say is merely sound
The dark night of the soul is here
Empty of comfort, filled with fear
The silent God is absent it is clear.

There's this shadow where a shadow shouldn't be
It's really there, but isn't really me.
There seems no kind of respite I can find
Half living, in the shadows of my mind.

Finding a Soul

'This me, that is to say the soul,
by which I am what I am'

(Rene Descartes)

'I can't see my life!' I said.
Sitting up in a bleak bed
to confront a hollow existence.
Disorientated, dismayed.
Destroyed.

She didn't understand.
Cared even less.

I cared though, and grieved
and was desperate.
But I didn't yet remotely understand
those peculiar words I'd said.
Coming as it seemed out of nowhere
to the nowhere I was just existing in.

There were recompenses even then
I suppose. But not that many.

Like being an observer of those so-called Swinging '60s.
But nothing to tell me who I was
Or why it mattered.

I needed to overturn my life
even to begin to understand.
And start the confusing journey
from un-being, to being
a 'who' as opposed to just a 'what'.
To find my meanings and start
to live them however precariously.

I found my first clue in the lovely
and beloved form
of a woman who did care about me –
and about who I might have the potential to be.
Her soul carried mine to a sweeter place.

But even with the deepest of loves before you
there turns out to be no easy pathway.

To totally find your soul
first you have to bare it to yourself
and watch it bleed
in the presence of a trained, objective stranger.

And that turns out to be
merely the first step
in an even longer journey
from sickness to health.

Gradually, painfully, to come to terms
with who this new self that's me
might be yearning to be.
When seen through other eyes,
Those of the all-seeing Other
who is beyond my comprehension.

I'm realising every day that coming home
to understanding who I truly am
is turning out to be
the longest journey I have ever taken.

And I'm still far away from home,
not even approaching
the general neighbourhood.
But at least I finally know
where 'there' is.
Even if I'm not yet capable
of getting there.

And now I can finally see my life,
if most often only dimly.
So that helped by the one I love
and the One who loves me,
I hope I'm slowly stumbling
towards a destination.

Recognising that this travel-stained soul
is the true 'I am' that was always 'Me'.
Now in search of the end that is only
its beginning.

*'Theology is the attempt to say
the least stupid things about God'
(inspired by a lecture by Rowan Williams)*

The Problems of Theology

Isms and ologies
Vacuous tautologies
These are the fate
Of those who create
Polysyllabic apologies.

Must it be so?
Can we not grow
Out of such childish mythologies?
Knowing at last
That 'The First And The Last'
Is untouched by our stale theodicies.

Better by far
To remain as we are
In a state of inchoate confusions
Than to torture our minds
With ineffable kinds
Of perplexed and recursive illusions.

Beyond Words

I have no words to tell you
even remotely what I mean
when I claim to love you.
I, who cannot even know you.

Anything that I strive to say
dissolves into feeble failure.
Only able to diminish
what it describes.

So to speak at all is to make a choice
between the absolute made ordinary –
or just a muffled defeat.
'Of that whereof we cannot speak,
thereof we must remain silent.'
Easier not said than not done.
Unfortunately – or thankfully?

I don't know where
any words could usefully begin
to describe your love for me.
Or that it will never end.

'I am with you to the end of the age'
is the nearest I can get to it.

So maybe I can only pay you back
in the silence that lives
at the other side of speech.
In the worship that lurks
within the breath
that cannot be exhaled.

Leaving me gasping to articulate,
to swallow the uncertainty.
Lost in a kind
of spiritual suffocation.

One in which I'm only able to insist
silently and oh so painfully
that your love for me
lies way beyond the reach and resonance
of human speaking.

And yet a love that's strong enough
to have survived
each shameful thing I've said and done.

The promises I've broken.
Each carefully varnished lie.
The diminution of your truth
into mere truism.
Each all too easy betrayal
of your holy Word.

Without words there can be
no human defence
and no acquital.
But where words fall silent
there is maybe no need
for any of that after all.

Instead we just must trust
in the aspiration. The inspiration.
The affirmation.
Decisive actions that will send
those superfluous words
scurrying back to where they belong
in the place of their unsaying.
Leaving behind a certainty
that remains strongest when unspoken.

And so I have no words,
there are no words.
And none are needed.
Except for the Word that lives
behind, beyond, beneath, above
all other words.

And is alone the Word of God.

Nothing Left

There's nothing left in my heart
Just dryness where blood was
A desert where hope was

Nothing left.

There's nothing left in my soul
Smothering dullness
No vestige of fullness

Nothing left.

Water my heart
Pour into my soul
Banish these remnants
Come make me whole

Wholly alive

Don't leave me confused
Bruised and misused
crushed and discarded
Like yesterday's garbage

Show me the way

Fulfil your promise
Of life ever after
Turn off the weeping
Turn on the laughter
Remake me now

Into a new thing
Beloved and true thing
Loved and protected
Not abandoned, neglected.

Bless me again

Cradled and nurtured
Quietly blessed
If you are here with me
Be damned to the rest.

For wrapped in your mercy
No one is left.

Out of Sight, Out of Mind?

The children of my imagination
are squalling in the distance.

Locked out of sight and hearing
safe in the prison of my hard drive.

They want to speak and be spoken about.
Preferably to be cuddled and told

you are wonderful.
No wonder Daddy loves you.

But what if I let them loose upon the world
and they behave badly?
Sound childish. Act needy.
Say things that only a parent could love?

Would I blame them?
Blame the world?
Or simply blame myself?

Ashamed for having offspring
so badly brought up?

Even as I write I can hear them
crying themselves back to sleep.

It would be a pity if they
never got their moment
in the sun.
Or got the chance to hold hands
as they crossed the road.

Unless theirs turned out to be
just a brief life of shame.

Maybe better to get no response
than the response that
every parent dreads to hear.

Your babies are ugly.

On Christmas Eve

This night is like no other night
The overarching empty sky
Is full of an approaching joy
That we must not pass by.

He holds our lives in tiny hands
Child of all times and seasons
Our brightest future, darkest past,
In deeply hidden reasons.

We are like children once again,
This holy night now shows us
How innocence, how loving arms
Can evermore enfold us.

Oh may we stay, as now we pray,
In peace that ends our aching,
Cradled within God's tender care
In sleeping and in waking!

Old Bach

They said
you were finished.
Out of fashion.
'Old Wig' they called you.
Yesterday's man.

Not the kind of stuff
the young folks
want to hear
nowadays

Pedagogue and pedant,
filed under
'way back when'.

Still useful for students
to practise on
but not inspiring.

And yet
from within that
infinite mind
still sprang

a bottomless
well of beauty.

Transcendent
truths, only to be
comprehended
by us, over time

'I write down the notes but
God makes the music'
you said.

'Solo Dei Gloria.
For the glory of God alone.'

And so you still speak
to us now.

While the fashionable
others have vanished

into well-deserved
obscurity.

But you still sing within us.
Turning complex thought
Into audible beauty.

Mathematical tangles
Into cadences
that speak beyond speech

of God's mystery.

You show us that
what can only be seen
is no more than a rumour
of all that exists.

For that we thank you,
and the One
who formed you
into an everlasting
testimony to Grace.

Grace made audible,
Transfigured
into sound.
To the glory of
God alone.

Noli Me Tangere

What does it mean to someone to be touched?
What does it demonstrate about ourselves?

It reassures us that we still exist.
A body that remains within a world
Of bodies. Blood bone warmth response.
The reassuring otherness of others.
It touches us emotionally above all.
In giving and receiving love.

Without that touch we shrivel till we cease.
Become unmanned unwomanned and unmade.

So living in a world where touch is cancelled
Where distance leaves us physically bereft
Holds us apart from all our natural instincts.
Leaves us marooned in our own private pool
Of absent loneliness.

And yet our own survival seems to rest upon
This deadening sense of being on our own.
No matter how we look at it we suffer
Either by absence or by stolen joys.

'Noli me tangere,' said Christ to Mary.
'Don't try to touch me now,' he gently warned
Deprived the one who ached and mourned that morning
Of that life-giving touch of someone lost
Whose words and ways and warm propinquity
Had changed her life to plenitude from poverty.
As it was then for faithful grieving Mary
This time of waiting feels beyond all bearing.
Waiting for when our tentative outstretching
Touches the One whose resurrection blessing
Transcends all loss and pain forevermore.

And through the broken body that he offers
Like Thomas we may unexpectedly
Touch not just others, but Eternity.

My Chance at Love

I didn't sense that you were there
I didn't even dare to look.
I found no meaning anywhere
My hopes were a closed book.

So many things got in the way
The worldly voices were too loud.
The whispers of your love for me
Were drowned out by the crowd.

(Chorus)

You are to me my second chance,
My bond of love, my holy dance.
Be with me as I seek your face
And strain to stumble into Grace.

Yes now at last I'm changing fast
And praying that I'll be forgiven.
I hear you now, and ache to claim
My chance of love, my hope of heaven.

My loving Lord, my God above
Enfold me in your arms of love
Receive me as I seize my chance
To live, within your endless dance.

(Final Chorus)

You are to me my second chance,
My bond of love, my holy dance.
Stay with me as I seek your face
And strain to stumble into Grace.

A Kind of Pleading

'O Lord hear my prayer
O Lord hear my prayer
When I call answer me.'

(Taize chant)

So why don't you?
You who know all things
know that I call
from the depths of despair.

But you only offer your silence in return.
Is this to teach me a lesson
I who never called on you
when I needed for nothing?

Or is it an invitation to grow up
and be mature in Christ
as Paul so confidently called it?
Whatever the reason
the silence is destroying me.

You have all my attention now
although I don't seem to have
any of yours.

Tell me who can I turn to
if you turn away?
If I am nothing to you
then maybe I am simply nothing.
To you or anyone.

So why taunt me with your existence.
Why tell me of your loving kindness
that is unreachable. Or at least
not on offer to me.

Perhaps my pleading embarrasses you
as much as it embarrasses me.
Happy and shiny I should be.
Not hopeless and lifeless.

So maybe your will
is like some bitter pill
that I must either swallow.
Or choke on.

Maybe that's what my life's
supposed to be about.

Meaning that even if you can
so steadfastly ignore my pleas
still at the very least
my pleading pleases you.

'I Think You're Somebody
I Used to Love'

Think. Again.

Somebody loved by.

Who then?

Used to. When?

Love lost. Gone just.

Who? Me?

But who me?

Was like you
was like me

What now
that used to be?

Nothing there
if not called me.

What bit still
of what is me?

Touching? Feeling?
Loving? Free?

No it's over.
lost and over

Love. Me.

Some Body.

Siren Voices

Johannes Brahms and Leonard Cohen
Their siren voices keep me going
One sounds out beauty from personal pain
The other confesses again and again.

Each builds their passion from ordinary life
Freedom in loneliness, a lost lover or wife
Turning each insight on future or past
Into passion and beauty whose relevance lasts.

One sings out his heart to a god he can't find
The other asks questions that seethe in his mind
Of a god who is silent, who mostly belongs
In the agonised wonderings of his greatest songs.

They minister to us each from their own pain
Defining who we are again and again.
So what am I left as? The tiniest part
Of something I dare not call talent or art.

A rejected adagio, a figure of fun,

An ill-tuned piano, a verse just begun.

Though I strive to keep up yet I know all the time

I'm no more than an old man who knows how to rhyme.

Outer Darkness
Inner Light

'As the circle of light increases,
so does the circumference of darkness'
(attributed to Albert Einstein)

Is this some huge spiritual insight
about the cosmic struggle between good and evil?
Or just an obvious factual truism?
Profound, or merely self-evident?

On the one hand no more than
a low-key scientific observation
straining too hard to stray
into the world of philosophy.

But on the other hand maybe an essential insight,
pointing us towards knowledge of the God
who does not play dice!

It would be reassuring to believe
that these two paradoxical interpretations
could somehow meld into one huge discovery.
One that can make reality clearer to us.

But too often the evidence seems to support Einstein's dictum
in a tragically negative way.
Given that darkness seems to spread its rule
through the merciless grip of entropy.
So here we stand,
marooned within an unresolved conflict.
One between what there is and why there is.
A contradiction that has for evermore
haunted all those who look for meaning.
If only just a tantalising clue
to what could be, but may not be.
True.

When we confront the darker implications
Of Einstein's spreading darkness
it can all too often feel
that worldly reality and God's justice move
in contradictory directions.

The faithful suffer
the faithless thrive.
Truth struggles to find its voice
while falsehood shouts it down.

A scandal that the psalmists felt,
as they mourned and railed against
all those blood-soaked
stumbling blocks to faith
that we still suffer from.

Accusing, like them,
the God who seems to manifest himself
mostly as an absent rumour.
Or more positively,
the One who can be loved
but never known.

Now maybe that's the stiff and rusted key
that unlocks the meaning.
That the light of Christ must constantly fight
against the insidious penumbra of evil
that always works to drag us down
into a deeper darkness.

So that we sometimes feel ourselves
helpless observers of a cosmic battle
that is beyond our understanding.
One that nobody seems to be winning.

So where can we turn for clarity?
The tough truth is, probably nowhere.
We cannot know what by definition
cannot be known.
And maybe that's the point.
Perhaps the answer hides,
Buried deep inside the question.
Within God's healing darkness.

So that just as Einstein could only hypothesise
about what could never be known for sure
so we can only adore and worship
that which we can never fully know.

Not despite our lack of knowing
but because of it.

So let us step back from
that circumference of darkness.
And stay forever in the circle of light
that is God's mercy.

Unknowable, but unending.

Now but Not Yet

'I don't want it to be over'.
Words torn out of your grief.

I dread the thought of everything I was
dissolving into nothing.
Nothing cannot live or love.

Will it arrive as
a tiptoeing deceptive sleep
that has no wakening?

Or shameful struggle
desperate huddle
anguished muddle
a soul-bent double?

And as for you my love
my heart aches now for what you lose
all those dear things that filled our happiest days.

The passion, closenesses,
the sweet epiphanies.
All gone. Instead only a vacuum.

Does love survive our deaths or simply fade?
We who were one, imprisoned then
in never-ending separation?
Lost and directionless as when we met?
Is there a place for us as sweet as here?
A love as all-encompassing as this?
I used to think so, now I can't be sure.
Mired in the uncertainty I had before.

I have to be prepared to be no more.
And yet I'm not.
'Not yet.
No. More.'

Night Thoughts

They call it stolen time,
'tempo rubato'.
As if the pianist borrowed time
from God.
And brought it back
to you and me,
newly blessed.

Left hand and right hand
move at opposing speeds
across the keyboard,
as if fleeing from each other.
Only to be reconciled
into a new and deeper union,
at the end of each phrase.

This is Chopin's world,
the world of his Nocturnes.
Night thoughts that turn into
waking dreams.
Singing of a reality
that can only ever be
experienced by us

outside of time.

Some condemned these night thoughts
as the music of seduction.
An understandable but
inadequate description.
They show us so much more
than human mingling.
The Nocturnes are seductions,
for sure, but of the heart and soul,
Chopin's and ours.
Newly bound to each other
in a more perfect act of love.

The greatest pianists have always
tested themselves
against the black and the white
of these keyboards of night.

Horowitz, the noblest of pianists,
claimed that rubato was a skill
that could never be taught.
It was either manifest
in the soul as well as the fingers.
Or it was beyond a musician's reach forever.

These nocturnes,
conversations with darkness,
brighten the night,
lighten the life.
Their murmurings

fly up from the keyboard
and back to us.

Searching their way to
the still centre of our
emotions. Then rising up, even to
the waiting ears of God.
Through their wanderings
we are made aware
of a deep and holy
peace within the soul
that nothing else
in life, or even in much music,
can shower upon us.

Brief as a Nocturne is
each one reminds us,
time after time,
that God's eternity
is of a perfect beauty
that transcends time.

And they invite us
to transcend time for ourselves
in the humbling,
healing, laying on
of the pianist's hands.

Not Enough

To say that I was smitten when I met you
And longed to have you wanting me as well
Cannot express what happened at that moment
It's not enough.

That first sweet touch that changed my life forever
The honesty the passion that we knew
Isn't a feeling words can ever measure
They're not enough.

Living together was a revelation
Where head and heart and body met to bless
The one who'd never known a loving woman
No way that I can thank you is enough.

When sudden sorrows came to us in legions
They seemed to pull us closer not apart
Like two strong trees that twine against the weather
The strength we found and shared – it was enough.

And now my darling, my life's love and centre
We have grown old yet all that was survives
For nothing can be lost that love has given
It always was, and always is, enough.

I pray that when the moment comes to sever
Your last touch that I feel, your tender voice
Will drift me out of life leaving us waiting
For shared eternity, more than enough.

Mocking Ourselves with Falsehood

Every serious word we utter is
a confession of a kind
of who we are.
Agonised unconscious
imperfect incomplete

A stuttered defence before the judge
who judges with a mercy
that can feel terrifying
in its wordlessness

Or so it seems to us
who only trade in words.

And betray ourselves each time
mocking ourselves with falsehood.
Though maybe even more guilty
in our endless furtive silences.

By which we hope to escape responsibility
for our deepest betrayals.
Because we reckon they are

too locked up within us
ever to be enunciated.

Either way we put ourselves at
the mercy of a Confessional
that we can no more escape
than we can comprehend it.

At our most honest struggling
to capture our truth
rather than wriggling to escape it.
The out-breathing from the epiglottis
our only weapon in a never-ending war of words.

Yet always our relentless chattering
confronts the Eternal Word.
that was in the beginning and shall be
at every Ending.

That spoke Creation and that speaks Salvation.
The cleansing Word that cares to stoop
and absolve our incoherent confessions.

So that despite our fear of dereliction
fallen flesh and Holy Spirit may someday
embrace. Knowing the strain and shame
and yet the glory. Of words.

'That Yonder'

(Damascius the Neo-Platonist.
On naming God)

Of all the names for God
the circumlocutions, the evasions
the euphemisms that shy away
from open voicing

This is surely the most subtle attempt
at saying the unsayable.

'That Yonder'.
The Unnamable Namer

The definition that says everything
by saying nothing.

The working titles of
that One Who Is.
Yet isn't. Ever to be
fully identified.

Presence in absence.
There. Out yonder.

Or somewhere.
Known only through being
unknowable Being.
Who can impossibly be
that One who dwells yonder?
wherever yonder may be hiding
from us?

'That Yonder' who wills that
even the inarticulate
shall nonetheless be saved?

That will take his dumbstruck people
up to the yonder that remains till now
his sealed-from-us sanctuary.

Can He be that same Yonder
that we shall someday find closer
rather than yonder?

If the Yonder that we ponder
cares to ponder about us?

It seems unavoidable that
if he was closer
rather than yonder
then we should have to define
what it is we cannot even describe

As it is, as He is
and will always be.

Let Him remain
the source and place of wonder.

'That Yonder'. Not here, but yonder.

The Body and the Blood

When all the words are spent the doctrine done
We kneel before his throne to meet the One
Who for our souls the ultimate of pain
Embraced, and undefeated rose again.

His sacrifice is given without end
To warm all hearts, all broken lives to mend
He's with us now as he was with us then
Kneeling beside us as we kneel again.

Takes on His Cross the weight of all our sin
Carries the heaviness that locks us in
In Him is all the lightness that we need
The grace, the glory, through His wounded deed.

The bread is him, the wine his sacred blood
Reality suspended so we could
Taste His great gift in body and in blood
Through His pure love share in that greatest good.

And so it's over, all is sacred now
And yet when we are asked we can't say how
This holy and eternal glory given

Transforms us as we touch the edge of heaven.

Until we taste that sacred moment when
We share the body and the blood again.

Sorrow and Love

'When I dreamed of love
it turned to sorrow.
And when I dreamed of sorrow
it turned to love.'

So wrote Schubert to his brother.
And that perplexity was dramatized
in everything he wrote.

The relentless tramp in the bass line
Of the wanderer who knows himself
to be homeless in this world.

The slow surreal drift of the adagios
that capture in eddies of sound
that strange moment before a faint.

And then the bonhomie,
Gemutlichkeit they call it,
Of the scherzos that invite us
To dance away our sorrows.
Until the next time.

His music was the outcome
of his love. But sadly not the only one.
Some of the others left him syphilis,
Which cost him an early death.

Ironic that the gift that killed him
Should also give him immortality.
That those last six months
wracked by dissolution
should have led him to
his greatest inspirations.

Cryptic sonatas, quartets, a quintet,
a Great C Major symphony.
Were they coded messages of
a last, loving, goodbye?

He could not have known that
in his love and sorrow,
his joys and desperation
he would give us

deeper meaning for all of those
moments that show us what it means
to be human.

Yet without his inspiration
our joys and sorrows would have
been left at a loss,
with only lesser voices
to sing our meanings.

Stripped of their peaks and troughs,
their highs and lows,
their sorrows and loves,
Lives are lived less urgently.
Or simply matter less.

The Eternal Now

'There's no before or after in the Scriptures
All time resides in God's eternity.'

So say the Rabbis, knowing more than I do
Aware that what we experience as time
Is simply God's surveillance of our lives
That wields a temporal sovereignty upon us.
Though hours and years and decades that we live
Are just a tiny sliver of God's always.

The Son of Man, our Saviour born in time
But timeless too before time was brought forth
Sent by the One who is the Lord of Time
Lives on in history and eternity.
Time past, time present, and time future, run
A thousand ages like an evening gone.

Then why protest the passing of our years?
Why kick against the intolerable end?
Can we not see that all that we can see
The ending that we shrink from in our fear
Is indistinguishable from our beginning
In God's all-comprehending loving mind?

Our lifespan's just a foretaste of eternity
Each life enfolded in the mind of God
Until we stand before the timeless Father
Who is the Son and Spirit, three in one.
No longer tangled in before and after
But held where who we were and are shall be
Eternally and blessedly all one.

The 'I' That Isn't 'You'

Who is this one that is described as I?
Who is that other one described as you?
Fragments, no more, of two sequestered selves
That can't determine who or what is true.
About that me that knows it isn't you.

We prowl alone a world of dark unknowing
A world that Freud knew deeply and too well
Troubled by dreams, the horror of un-being
An incoherence, true of Me and You.
In gloom the light of logic can't pierce through.

While down below the atavistic self
Rages and weeps, immune from thought or help.
Just an occluded fragment of a self
Loosely composed of faltering intuition
Combined into a haunting, blurry vision

Of who I am and how it feels to be
No more than some isolated promontory.
And less what it might even mean to be
A You or a Me.

Is this the way it has to be?
Is it the same for you as it's for me?

Life is little more than just
An arbitrary state of flux
Purposeless, bereft of meaning.
We hear philosophers still believing.
At best a fibrillating mess
That masquerades as consciousness.

If so, is God just childish supposition
The 'Great I Am' simplistic superstition?

Not so. Sheer absence gives the strongest clue
To that Power that created Me and You.

Our unimaginable heartfelt longing
That's stronger than all human bonding.

The hope we share, the selves who strain
To know and love each other,
All held within the greater love of that great Other.
As God perfects our final 'I' and 'You'
And all that is unknown, and yet is true.

The Gift

Just what I always wanted
We smile and lie and say
When what is given is rejected
The price of gratitude
Too steep to pay.

The problem is we don't know what we want
Only that it must come to us in love
But love and value aren't the same it seems
So love is never valued or acknowledged
anything like enough.

The Christian view of life as gift
has poignant similarity
We take the gift, resent the price
Cannot accept what's offered us
And then refuse to pay the fee.

How little we value the gift from Him
Who gave his all for those
Who sneered and snarled, blasphemed and tore
The One whose love had offered them
His life and so much more.

Our only response is to cling to the hope
Of the gift of eternal living
So that someday we'll value the love in the look
And the price that it took
From the Giver whose love keeps on giving.

Stranded Between Worlds

He seems to have lived in a state of
constant contradiction
between the life and the music.
Or that's how it feels when we hear him
sing to us from his soul.

Letting us into his innermost self
and its insights.
A place that was normally
Out of bounds to strangers.

Nurtured by the distant past,
He found it still present and alive
in Schutz and Bach and Palestrina.
And made their disciplined,
compelling tread his own
particular signature.

Their regularities, their cadences
and their solemnities became his.
He wore them like a favourite coat.
One that has many unimagined
colours hidden in its lining.

Haunted as he was by
the rupture of the musical
tradition that Wagner committed,
he found his own ways to innovate.
Looking backwards and forwards
simultaneously, like the god Janus.
Piano works that blazed
with carefully calibrated discords,
or sank into what he called
'cradle songs for my sorrows'.
The intricate interstices
of Fugue and Passacalia
from other ages,
breathed into new life for this one.
In symphonies and chamber works
that seemed to move
from understatement
into rapturous glowing.

He saw himself too as the inheritor
of a more recent tradition,
one that terrified him.
And the main source of this terror
being the looming presence of
dead Beethoven.
What had he left
for anyone else to say?

Fear of failure made him deprive our ears
of innumerable false starts.
Before he finally made peace

with his art in a way that
he could never achieve
in his own life.
Wounded forever by
who he had been.
Born in rough unfashionable Hamburg.
Giving his first public performances
while still a child. In places dedicated
to other kinds of performance.
The city's brothels.

The kindly women there introduced him
to the mystery of bodies.
Not knowing that by doing so
They would leave him unable
to commit his own to love.
Only to lust.

A wound that left him only fantasising
the unapproachable, unattainable Clara
all his life. Everything he wanted
but didn't know how to ask for.

His life motto says it all:
'Frei Aber Einsam'.
Free but lonely.
And that loneliness,
that inability
to connect with life
except in the noisy anonymity
of beer halls, turned his life sour.

But gave him the space to turn
his bitter life experiences
into sweet genius.

Searching for what cannot ever be found
Is a pretty good definition of great art.
Or at least it's a good place to start searching.
When I hear Brahms I hear the strains
Of desolation, intermingled
with the rhapsody of loving and longing.
Our blessing is to share with him in music
The love he couldn't share with anyone.
Because the man who never
fully knew himself in life
is the one who, in his music,
knows me like no other ever can.

What I Started to Say

Already I feel myself veering away
from what I thought I had in mind to say.
That's the trouble with thoughts you see.
They wriggle, double back, hide from you.

Then flit away when you're not looking.
Start sentences all on their own.
Some irrelevant or at a tangent
to what you had intended.
Some downright discreditable
even disgusting.

I thought today I'd like to be
solemn and sententious,
That's what my conscious mind had in mind.
But my unconstrained unconscious
had other ideas, if you can call them that.
Glib and innocuous they turned out to be.
Miles away from what I planned to say.

That's how sentences are you see.
They play Russian roulette with the writer.
You never know which one will explode in your face

and bring a sudden end to what you meant to say.

Or else just click harmlessly into inconsequence.
Leaving us feebly claiming
that's what we meant to tell you all along.

But the truth is nothing like that.
The sentences scamper off without permission
to live a brief unauthorised life without us.
Leaving us with the problem of starting over.
And over. Ever further away
from what we'd started to say.

You don't ever know
where a sentence will slip away to.
Often it's far from where you wanted to go.
But sometimes, just sometimes, you find yourself
somewhere you could never have conceived of being.

A dizzying plateau of sentences where
there is no pressure and the air is fresher.
And once there we can sit a while and savour
such a rare victory as makes the rest worthwhile.
Before we have to stumble back to earth
and wrestle with the next undignified defeat
that's bound to follow.

Funeral of a Solipsist

The great thing about my funeral
will be that I shall be
the centre of everything.

As I always have been,
but now in death as in life.

I'll make sure everything goes
exactly the way I want it to.
A celebration of me
and everything about me.

Because me is all there is
and was. Will be
or could be.

Me and my uniqueness
My multitude of talents.
My overwhelmingly irresistible charm.

The impact I would have had
on everyone around me

were it not that nobody else
has ever actually existed
to celebrate me as I deserve to be.

So there won't be anybody around
to mourn. And even if there was
they would miserably fail to imagine
a world without me
any more than I can you see.

Because philosophically speaking
even to try to conceive of nothingness
would be an impossibility.
A crass Category Error.

So I can only give imaginary life
to these non-existent others
weeping, singing, mourning keening

Or at least doing their best to,
despite their inconvenient non-existence.

I plan to choose all the hymns
Vet the readings
to ensure suitable self-centredness.

Legislate sufficiently solemn music
the kind that would bring an imaginary tear
to non-existent eyes as they all sat

devastated and speechless
in that illusory congregation.

It's going to be a great occasion.
Though sadly (whatever sadly means)
without the only person who would have
enjoyed it the most,

The be all and end all of all things,
as I know myself to have been,
will have finished being.
And will have come to a lonely end
leaving this world, my self-created world,

finally totally unarguably definitively.
Empty.

'You Are the Journey and the Journey's End'

from a prayer of Boethius

It sounds kind of
uncomplicated
when you put it
like that. So let me
put it this way
instead.

Are you ready
to walk with me
to the better place
which is this place,
but transformed?

To be my clumsy neophyte,
limping to keep up.
And yet the darling
of my bosom, resting
at my right hand?

Don't ask me why
I want you,

God alone knows why.
And that means
I should know too.
Because that's home
territory for me.
Anyway I suppose
I'm stuck with you
because of that promise
I made long ago.
'Until the end
of the age'.
My very words.

And that means I have
To watch you grow old,
as you continue
to miss the point
of everything I ever said to you.

And betray me
without even a thought.
Because you are
never thinking straight.

And yet I want you,
as well as watch over you,
on our journey.

Footsore, reluctant,
Holding on to the things
that I told you to

cast off aeons ago.

But the point is –
do you really want me?

You seem to find it
wearisome to make
room for me in your life.
Although I gave
mine for you.
Maybe you even resent it all,
and wish I'd leave you
in peace. Get off your case,
find someone else to prod.

If I was anyone else
I wouldn't bother
To drag you along
On this journey.

I'd cut my losses.
Find someone
more promising,
more malleable
maybe.

But in spite of everything
you are needed
on the journey.

And whatever
you may think of me now,
(assuming you even do),
you'll find me waiting
at the finishing line.

When you finally catch up.

Yesterday's Words

How can we claim originality
When everything we think and write must be
A tiny flake of someone else's truth?
Plagiarised unconsciously in the last week
Or dredged from memory of some childhood book.

It flatters us to see it as tradition
That we are part of culture's history
But what seems new to us is just a fragment
A titbit hardly worth a second glance
Spruced up in borrowed raiment for another chance.

There's no way out of this I'm sad to say
No thunderclap of genius right away.
For who we are and who we've been are one
With nothing radical to assault your ears
Nor anything new, under this same old sun.

So unashamedly we pick and steal
Detritus from our minds. For though we feel
The urge for innovation, revolution,
In fact we use tradition just to siphon
The truth we've learned from other poets' minds.

I find poets' confessions such a bore
As you must too, who've heard them all before.
So I promise you: when working day or night
I'll never stop to read before I write!

Waiting on God

You want to know
But you can't know
You get a glimmer
Then feel it go
Your faith is feeble
It just won't grow
While you're waiting on God.

Why can't it be
As clear as day?
Why can't the certainty
Come and stay?
No, you can't have it
Another way
Because you're waiting on God.

(Chorus)

But the time will come
Though it seems so slow
That faith will flourish
Not come and go
As we are known

So shall we know
After we've waited on God.

Some people claim
There's no one there
And if there is
What does he care?
For you and me
And all our prayer
As we're waiting on God.

Oh the day seems far off
The night moves slow
But as we are known
So shall we know
The darkness banished
By morning's glow
Now we've waited on God.

Up Here, Down There

It's really great up here
I hear it's shit down there
I promised you my help
But I don't really care.

Too busy now up here
To notice human fear
Full of my endless power
To make your life a poison shower.

So stop complaining
Although it's raining
With your hot tears
And paralysing fears.

It could be worse
I could fling a curse
Though that's not much different
From my impregnable indifference.

'Thoughts and prayers'
From the One who claims he cares.
Who calls you his friend
But deserts you in the end.

Wandering Through
the Dark Night of the Soul

There is a place where God cannot be found
There is no light there,
No delight there,
A state of nothingness that terrifies
Though we seek a way out
From inside that dark night
We feel lost in it only
Abandoned and lonely.

Wandering through
Our dark night of the soul.
Where God is out of reach.

We're not the first,
And we won't be the last
A host of sufferers, reaching back into the past
From Plato's prisoners, shrinking from the light
To Christ's opponents, blind to what was right
And blind John Milton's dream of love
Till day brought back his night.

Can we believe that dark night has an ending?
That God will share the light
That has no ending?
Will resurrection bodies heal again
The weight we drag, a crushing ball and chain?
Shall we reclaim the light in all its glory
Is there a hope beyond this hopeless story?
We must survive the sickness of the soul
Till God in his great mercy makes us whole
Until we see as we are seen, again
When God will quell the darkness and its reign.
We have to trust what God can do,
That He has promised what is true.
Leading us home, guiding us past
That dark night of the soul, at last.

The Ground
of Their Beseeching

Absolution.

I meet it most in music
reaching back in history
to the time of Byrd
and all his Catholic brothers
for calm considered sanity
against the odds.

And the odds were cripplingly high.
Because they lived all of them
in an age plagued by the curse
of murderous religious turmoil.

A time that fathered either
actual death or paralysing melancholy
if they so much as spoke aloud
their inner faith
in a forbidden language.

Doom and dreadful death snapped
at the heels of every Recusant.
So what could counteract their fears
and keep their motives pure?
Only a language that could not be
betrayed by words.

The seditious murmurings of music.

So those masters of the harmonic 'ground'
that steadied notes and chords
into an embrace
of unassailable private beauty
they brought all their beseeching into focus.

Kept their prayers private and inviolate
as they wrestled to defeat
the worst of all their perils.

Through the power of harmony.
Tentative, troubled, never tumultuous
but soaked in subterranean, understated grief
they gifted all they stood for
through their fingers.

Fingers that couldn't lie or be accused
of musical sedition.

And that is why their music speaks to us
We heal our insecurities through theirs.

Feast on the hunger that
their art transfigured.
Into a timeless truth no longer needing
to speak in words.

I know that letting loose their wordless beauty
for minutes only, can make up
for all my dangerous hours of ugly speech.
And then I can return, briefly reborn
through the purification that
their music brings.

Because their sweet, tender beseeching
absolves me from the dangerous
tyranny. Of words.

Returning to the Light

(In memory of a musician)

Some people carry their darkness within them
Some overflow with pure light,
Their presence illumines the day that surrounds them
While the others lie stifled by night.

But is nothing left when their voices are gone
No more than vibrations of air?
Are we bereft of their sounds that we loved
Nothing still tangible there?

He was shy in his speech
But his fingers could reach
What he wasn't able to say
He stumbled and stuttered
But his words as they muttered,
Rang out when he started to play.

I tried with my voice
To give him the choice
Of some things that his music might say
But my words couldn't capture
His instinctive rapture

That said so much more anyway.
May his lightness ring out
May his Lord seek him out
For what his music was able to say
In that place where God's light
Knows nothing of night
But pours out without end every day.

*Lord, your music is a lantern unto my feet
and a light unto my path.*

These Dear Last Days

These dear last days that God has given
Let's live them as a taste of heaven.
To celebrate, to laugh at fate
Love till the last, no time to waste.
Relive those years we've lived and loved
Until we're called by God above.

The life that's here, the love we share
A foretaste of the love that's there,
God's love that bleeds, God's love that mends
Within the One who knows no end.
No sorrows left, just joyful hearts
Our end is where the new life starts.

Those dear last days that God has given
Let's live them as a taste of heaven.

The Sound of Sanity

Maybe this is the 'Equal Music'
that John Donne preached about.
The sounds that belong in Heaven.

Constant. Comforting in their
humanity, before the face of divinity.

Never out of kilter. Solid in substance.
Reminding us of our saner selves.

Yes, his music is the voice of
moderation, Of self-control.
Of sanity itself.

And yet this, his greatest strength,
is so often seen as limitation.

Meaning that
Haydn has been condemned to
live in a place called
the 'middle of the road'.

Included in concerts as
No more than the warm-up act
that comes before
the serious stuff.

How unjust and
unseeing we are.
His voice is no less strong for
its quiet self-understanding,
its unselfconscious raptures.

Compositions rooted in a tradition
that he constantly reinvents.
Always taking the best of the past with him
to thrive in new and broader pastures.

All the while as if to plead:
'I am just a music maker,
simply an artisan,
the servant of the Muse
And not her master.'

And so he produces,
with joy and humility
over so many years,
endless outpourings
of musical inventiveness.

Deep reflection, holy insight,
unbuttoned mirth.
Solemn, but never just

for solemn's sake.
Far away from severe.

And generous to a fault
With the faults of the new
generation.

Child Mozart the prodigy,
or the uncontrollable,
ungrateful Beethoven.
A life of service to music
and to the one demanding employer.
Cloistered away from fashion,
yet instinctively working
at the edge of quiet innovation.

Faithful to self and to God
even though a world away
from even the rumour of fame.

Until basking in an Indian summer
as they belatedly recognised
his seemingly limitless genius,
he quietly takes his natural position
At the top table of celebrity.
And from there he still invites us
to rest with him. While we recuperate
from the exhaustion of the world
that his music still finds a way
to lift us above.

In a society enslaved to madness,
now as then, his is the voice
of sanity that keeps calling me
back to him.

Whenever I ache for renewal.
And can summon up the sense
to simply sit and listen.

Your Will Not Mine

What I will for me is selfish and small.
What you will for me is selfless and endless.

My will grabs for what it wants and calls it freedom
Your will is conformed to what the Father wants,
and calls it love.

I am enslaved in the dungeon of my will
Your will is the service that is perfect freedom.

Will you ever forgive me for the ills that I will?
Will I ever give in to the good you will for me?

Will there ever be a world without end?
And will I ever be worthy to end up there?

Will I ever cease my willing?
Will you ever cease forgiving?

Lord your will not mine
And your will be done.

You Can't See Me Cry

We get on with our lives as best we can.
The days slip by, a blur for you and me.
We tell ourselves what's left can still make sense
And seek things that can serve as recompense
And you can't see me cry.

We tell ourselves it's slowly getting better
And over time we'll hardly feel what's gone
But when we think the other doesn't notice
We fall apart and mourn the life that's gone.
And you can't see me cry.

We dread the prospect of declining years
As one of us, or both, loses our strength
Our lives will be reduced, and we shall pine for
The quality, if all that's left is length
And you won't see me die.

Eventually we'll know the what and why,
Standing before the One who sees all things,
Our pains, our passions, weakness, everything
The angel voices and the praise that rings.

But until then the sky has fallen on us
And in the debris of our life below
My wounded brave and all-beloved darling
An ache-filled love is all that we can know.

And you can't see me cry.

I, Who Wasn't,
Am, and Yet May Be

It has to be enough
There is no more
In a world of absence
I strive to survive.

I who wasn't, am, and yet may be.

In the sight and hand of God
We flourish and die
Joining the infinite number
Of those already ceased.

Hiding from knowing it
And from ourselves
Too much to cope with
So we live to forget.

Acting as if
What we have been
And are now
Is all there is.

Yet we in God's time
Shall be raised up
Not razed to zero again. No more,
then evermore, or so we pray.
There is more than we can
Imagine. Or bear to know of.
That is the secret
God keeps to himself.

Until it is time to
Astonish ourselves
With the immortality
We never asked for.

Because we couldn't conceive
Of what it might be.
We who weren't, and are
And yet may be.

Walking in Heaven

*Thoughts on the Adagio
from Beethoven's Opus 106,
The Hammerklavier*

It is a long journey and he is still locked away
from the sounds that used to energise him.
Now straining just to hear
his failure to compose.

And we are there too, lost with him
in a shared sad silence.
An anguished absence
that surrounds us both.
As he wrestles with a year
of arid non-achievement
in which deafness has finally triumphed.

Now as the adagio begins
a tentative, inchoate stirring
is all that he can painfully produce
and all that we can hear.
Feeling even sadder
than the silence felt.

Like hearing someone
smitten by a stroke,
painfully relearning to speak.
Or watching a damaged body
walking again in baby steps.
But then he breaks through the silence
and the laboured notes
form into a retrieved renewed
and even greater beauty.

As the one who was imprisoned in a hell
of silence is now walking in a heaven
of harmony.

As we listen, the tentative,
timid succession of fractured notes
resolves itself into a new and unimagined beauty.
'In heaven I shan't be deaf,' he said
And here is a sweet and blessed foretaste
of that moment.

Forevermore each note and cadence
more heaven-scaling than before.

A gift more precious than
a human heart could ask for:
that through his music we and he
may walk in heaven,
blessed, whole and free.

You Never Prayed to Me

In all the troubles that you knew
Did you not understand
Through all those years your name was kept
Here on the palm of my hand?

Occasionally you'd come for help
Or plead for one more chance
Deep in the toils of a life that felt
A slow macabre dance.

You rarely thanked me for your joys
Or noticed my loving care
Except to touch and heal your pain
You knew I would be there.

But still you dared to speak of me
Assumed the right to teach
My loving kindness and my power
When you used to lead and preach.

You've never really known me child
Our conversations few
Reluctant, stilted, formalised

Anything but true.

Yet now you stand in front of me
Before my mercy seat
No explanation good enough
No rationale complete.
What can I do with a fool like you
Who deserves to be shown the door?
Whose tears flow fast, who prays at last –
But love you for evermore?

The Still Small Voice
That Calls Us Home

Elijah heard the crashing of the thunder
He felt the earthquake saw the blinding light
But God was not in any of these wonders
Inside the cave that was as dark as night.

Until within the echoing of silence
He heard the still small voice he'd always known
The voice that through the ages has pursued us
To bring us back, to call us to our home.

Instead of hearing Him inside ourselves
Are we just seeking God in the wrong place?
Are our impatient wanderings leading us
Away from recognising inward Grace?

(Chorus)

And so as wanderers we hide and roam
Until that still small voice calls us back home.

That home is like no other place
It has no state but inward Grace

Like a dear lover in the night
It comes to us and finds us out.

And it will find us, you and I,
Although we hide, although we fly
To hear or not is our free choice
When we are called by that sweet voice.

(Final Chorus)

No more like wanderers we'll hide and roam,
We'll hear that still small voice, calling us home.

The night may be long and full of sorrow
but joy comes in the morning
(Psalm 30 Verse 5 paraphrased)